# COOKING SEAFOOD

## SRI LANKAN STYLE

Recipes by Shyamali Perera

Series 3

# Copyright

# Disclaimer

The material presented in this book is for informational purposes only. Please note that some ingredients mentioned in this book might not agree with first time users and food tasters.

# Dedication

To everyone who lost their lives during the global pandemic COVID-19 of 2019-2020.

To everyone who offered their services daily, to help us live through these difficult times.

To John Perera, my paternal grandfather, who I never met because he couldn't survive the last global pandemic of 1920.

*May all souls departed, rest in peace, and be guided to the "Divine Light".*

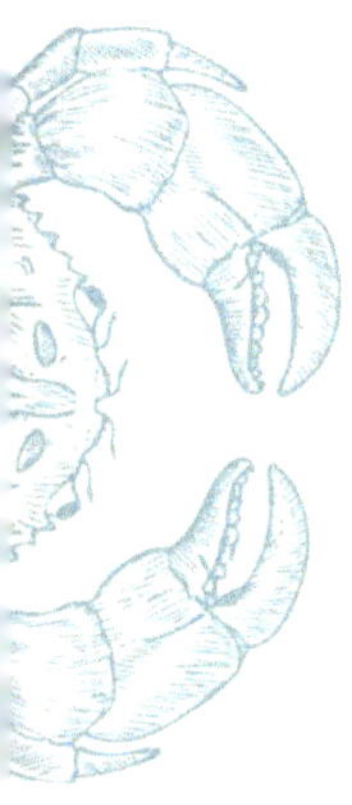

# TABLE OF CONTENTS

# INTRODUCTION

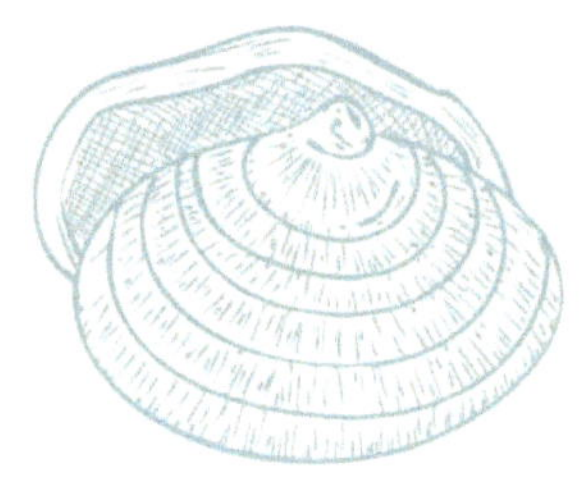

Ayubowan. Sri Lanka is a pear-shaped island tucked away in the Indian Ocean, below India. To the seventh-century Arabian spice merchants, it was known as Serendip, and to the European conquerors and explorers, Ceylon or the Pearl of the Indian Ocean. Sri Lanka boasts of not only a variety of climates but also well-adapted cultural influences.

Sri Lanka's history dates before the time of the Buddha when the aboriginal tribes of the Yakkas and the Nagas ruled the land and were a part of the ancient Asian civilization. It is chronicled in the Mahawansa that the Buddha visited Sri Lanka on several occasions in the fifth century BC to preach to these tribes amidst their ongoing wars. Although Sri Lanka has fought many battles during the past 2500 years, the island has been blessed with tropical beauty, an abundance of food and rare aromatic spices. Folklore and folk tales depict, that these rare herbs and spices as being brought to the island by the demigod Hanuman for medicinal purposes during the great battle between Ravana, the Yakka king, and the Hindu deity Rama.

A variety of spices and herbs are used in Sri Lankan cooking. But the cooking styles have a marked difference according to the region of origin. The north and east of the country have cuisines with prominent south Indian flavors, and the hill country is flavored with hill-grown fruits and vegetables. The west and coastal areas boast of cuisines with an abundance of fresh fish and vegetables.

The use of these spices can be considered a personal style and preference; therefore, exact measurements and quantities are deemed unnecessary. Hence the Sri Lankan cook throws in a pinch of this and a pinch of that and wham-bam......the outcome is mouth-watering food, layered with a multitude of flavors. The famous Sri Lankan curry refers to a variety of flavorful dishes cooked mostly with coconut milk and is eaten usually with rice. The recipes in this book are written with an international audience in mind and can be changed to suit one's palate.

*Hope you have a great culinary experience using these recipes.*

# ISSO-PRAWN CURRY

## Ingredients

50 jumbo prawns or shrimp
1 tbsp of chili powder
1/4 tsp of turmeric powder
4 pods of garlic chopped
2 slices of ginger chopped
2 inch cinnamon sticks
1 tbsp of oil
½ inch stem lemon grass
1 sprig curry leaves
½ tsp fenugreek
1 lime juice
1 cup thick coconut milk
salt to taste

## Directions

1 Wash the prawns well and set aside. Sauté the onions, garlic, ginger, curry leaves, cinnamon and fenugreek.
2 Add a little water to the thick coconut milk and mix with the sautéd onions. Then drop the prawns in, and cook for 5 minutes.
3 Lastly add the lime juice and salt. Serve when simmered and prawns are tender inside.

Notes. Please devein the prawn or shrimp before cooking.

# DALLO-DEVILED SQUID

## Ingredients

1 pound squid(cleaned)
1 medium white onion
2 green chilies
2 medium slices ginger
3 pods garlics
1 sprig curry leaves
1 inch pieces pandan leaves
1 tsp roasted curry powder
1 tsp chili powder
1 tsp turmeric powder
1 tbsp crushed red pepper
1 inch piece cinnamon stick
1 lemon
1/2 cup oil of your choice
salt to taste

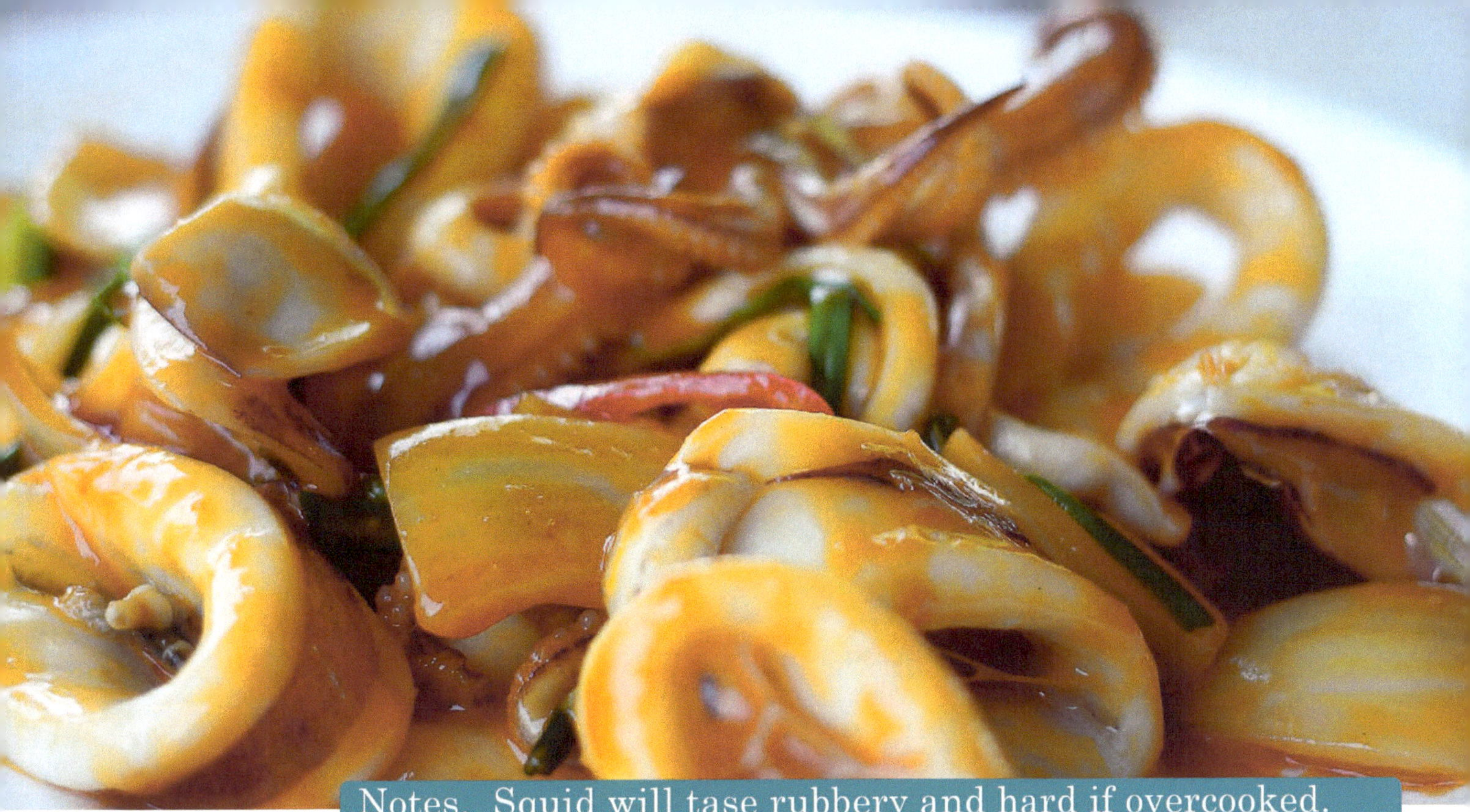

## Directions

1 Wash squid thoroughly with one half lime and water. Place in a colander to drain water. When drained cut squid into cubes. Set aside.
2 Chop the garlic, ginger and green chili finely, and slice the onion into rings. In a bowl mix the chopped garlic, ginger, onion rings with the turmeric, chili and curry powders. Add salt, curry leaves, pandan leaf and the cinnamon stick and leave for 5 minutes.
3 Heat oil in a deep fry pan and when oil is hot add the condiment mix and fry for 10 minutes until fragrant. Add squid cubes stir the mixture thoroughly for 5 minutes. Lastly add the crushed red pepper and stir well for 1 more minute.
4 Remove from heat and add the juice from the remaining lemon half. Mix well again so that the lemon juice is spread evenly. Serve hot.

# KAKULUVO-CRAB CURRY

## Ingredients

3 medium size crabs
2 ounces shallots
2 green chilies
3 pods garlic
3 slices ginger
2 tbsp grated coconut
½ tsp turmeric powder
½ tsp fenugreek
½ tsp chili powder
1 tsp curry powder
1 inch cinnamon stick
1 sprig curry leaves
1 ounce coriander leaves
½ inch stick of lemon grass
1 ¼ cup thin coconut milk
1 ¼ cup thick coconut milk
1 lime juice
2 tsp ground rice
salt to taste

# Directions

1 Place crabs in boiling water for 5 minutes, then remove and clean. Break the crab into desired portions and crush the shell a bit so the flesh can be easily removed.
2 Slice the shallots and chilies, grind garlic and ginger and grate the coconut.
3 Place the crab in a pan. Add the shallots, green chilies, garlic, ginger, fenugreek, turmeric, chili, paprika, and curry powders, curry leaves, cinnamon stick, coriander leaves, thin coconut milk and cook until crabs are tender and soft.
4 Mix the thick coconut milk with the lime juice, salt, grated coconut and the rice and add to the pan. Stir and simmer for about 10 minutes. Serve hot with roti or soft boiled rice.

Grated coconut is available at Asian grocery stores. This recipe is not for cooking live crabs.

MALU KIRI HODI-YELLOW FISH CURRY

## Ingredients

1 pound fish
1 onion
1/2 tsp turmeric powder
2 medium tomatoes
4 pods garlic
2 cloves
2 cardamoms
1 tbsp oil
1 inch cinnamon stick
¼ tsp chili powder
1 tsp paprika powder
1 tsp coriander powder
1 tsp fennel
1 cup coconut milk
1 lime juice
1inch lemongrass stem
1sprig curry leaves
Salt to taste

## Directions

1 Cut the fish into 8 pieces or as desired. Wash well pat dry, and sprinkle with salt, turmeric powder, and set aside.
2 Slice the onion and tomatoes, crush the garlic and powder cloves and cardamoms.
3 Heat the oil and when hot add the onion, garlic and curry leaves. Then add sliced tomatoes and cook for a few minutes.
4 Add the cinnamon stick, chili powder, paprika powder, coriander powder and fennel and cook for another few minutes.
5 Add the fish, mix in the coconut milk, salt, lemongrass, and cook until the fish is well cooked. Remove from the fire and sprinkle with lime juice when cool.

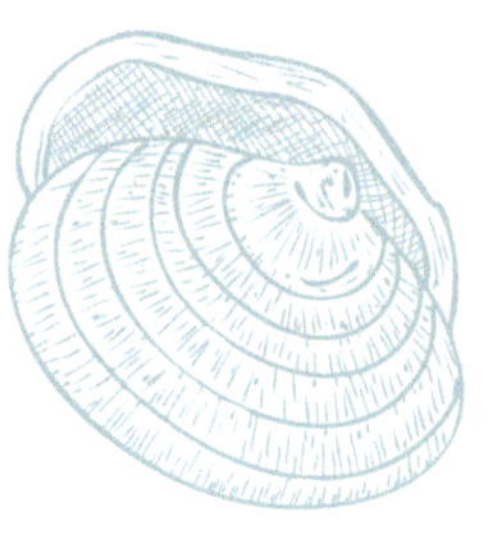

# MIRIS MALU-SPICY FISH CURRY

## Ingredients

1pound tuna or mahi mahi (or
any fish that can be cut into cubes)
1 tbsp chili powder
1 tbsp black pepper powder
4 pods of garlic
1 sprig curry leaves
1 inch cinnamon stick
2 tsp tamarind paste
1 tbsp of oil
½ cup of water
¼ tsp of turmeric powder
salt to taste

## Directions

1 Mix the fish with all the ingredients. Add oil, water and cook in high heat till the fish is well cooked and the gravy is very thick.
2 Serve with soft boiled rice, and any vegetable curry

# AMBUL THIYAL-SPICY PEPPER FISH

## Ingredients

1 pound tuna fish
4 pieces of goraka
1 tbsp peppercorns
1/4 tsp chili powder
1/4 tsp turmeric powder
3 garlic cloves
2 medium pieces ginger
1 inch pandan leaf
1 sprig curry leaves
1 lime juice
1/2 cup water
salt to taste

Dried Goraka

*Ambul Thiyal does not need to be refrigerated and can be kept out in an airtight box for 3 days.
*Flake the pieces of fish to make a tuna salad or tuna sandwich.
* Goraka:. Garcinia Cambodia.

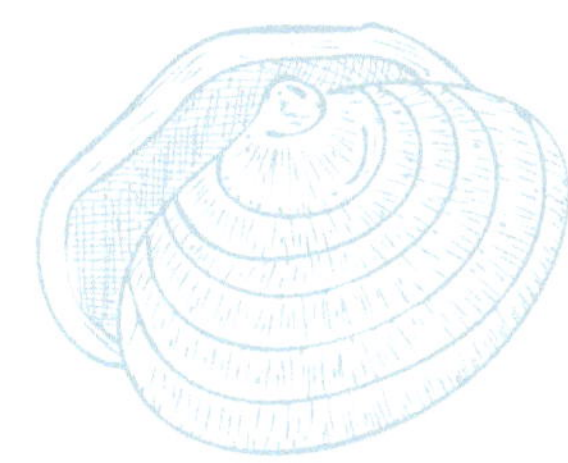

## Directions

1 Wash and soak goraka in hot water for about 30 minutes, till they become soft. Then puree the goraka, salt and peppercorns in the 1/2 cup water till it's a thick paste and set aside.

2 Cut the tuna fish into cubes and wash with the lime juice and water and leave to drain well. Add chopped garlic, ginger, chili powder, turmeric powder, pandan leaf, curry leaves to the fish and mix well.

3 While mixing make sure the pieces of fish are not smashed or flaked. Add the puree to the fish till the pieces are covered well. Add a tablespoon of water if the puree mixture is too thick.

4 Cover the pan and cook in medium heat for 15-20 minutes. Make sure the gravy does not dry up and burn. When cooked, the fish gravy should be thick and the fish soft and pinky.

# SALMON CURRY

## Ingredients

1 can salmon or mackerel
1 onion chopped
1 tbsp chili powder
1 tbsp of curry powder
2 pods of garlic
2 slices of ginger chopped
1 sprig curry Leaves
1 inch stem lemon grass
½ tsp fenugreek
1 tbsp pepper powder
1 tbsp oil
½ inch piece of cinnamon
lime juice to taste
salt to taste

## Directions

1 Heat the oil and fry the onions, garlic, curry leaves, lemongrass, ginger, fenugreek and the cinnamon stick for about 5 minutes taking care not to burn the condiments.
2 Then add chili, pepper, curry powders. Empty the liquid from the can onto the fried ingredients and bring it to boil.
3 Next, add the fish and cook on low heat. Add lime juice on top.
4 Do not spoon the salmon constantly to form flakes.
5 Serve hot with bread or rice.

# HAL MASSO BADUN - FRIED ANCHOVIES

## Ingredients

1 pound fresh anchovies
1 tbsp chili powder
1 tsp turmeric powder
1 cup lemon juice
10 dried chilli
1 sprig curry leaves
3 cups oil
2 cups all purpose flour
1 cup water
Salt to taste

## Directions

1 Clean and wash the anchovies with water and 1/2 cup lemon juice. Drain in a colander till water is drained well. Then add the chili and turmeric powders and salt. Mix well and set aside.
2 Mix the flour, water, salt in a mixer to make a smooth creamy batter.
3 Heat oil, and dip a handful of marinated anchovies in the flour batter and slowly drop into the heated oil. Fry till golden brown. Repeat process till all the anchovies are fried.
4 Lastly reduce heat and fry the curry leaves and the red chili for about 1 minute.
5 Add the curry leaves and fried red chili to the anchovies and mix well before serving.

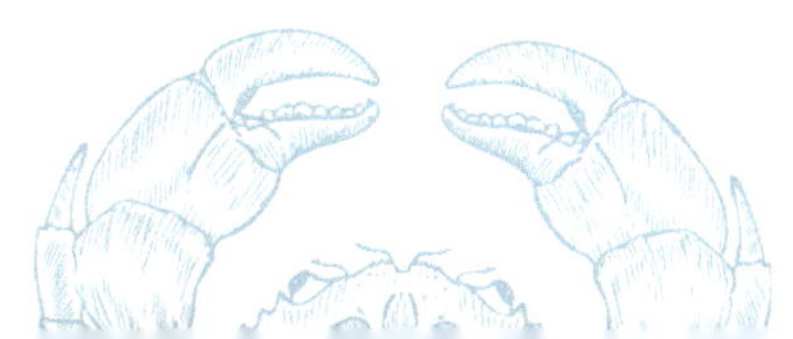

# KARAVALA BADUN-DEVILED SALTED DRIED FISH

## Ingredients

1/2 pound karavala (salted dried fish)
1/2 pound shallots
6 green chili
2 tsp crushed chili peppers
2 tsp lemon juice
1/2 cup oil
1 inch piece of pandan leaf
1 sprig curry leaves

Karavala

# Directions

1 Cut the karavala into small pieces and soak in lukewarm water for about 15 minutes till the pieces are soft. Wash thoroughly and pat dry.
2 Wash and cut shallots and green chilies finely. Heat oil and fry the shallots, till they soft and brown. Then add the pandan leaf, curry leaves and chopped green chili and fry for another 2 minutes. After 2 minutes of frying transfer the onion mix to a bowl.
3 Fry the karavala in the same pan for about 10 minutes till the oil is absorbed into the karavala pieces.  Reduce heat and add the fried onion mix, while stirring well for 2-3 minutes. Turn off the heat and add the crushed chili peppers and lime juice, and serve while hot.

# ACKNOWLEDGMENTS

Writing a book is harder than I thought and more rewarding than I could have ever imagined. None of this would have been possible without my awesome 86 yr old mother, Nalini Perera. She was the narrator for this series of Sri Lankan recipes during our mandatory quarantine for the COVID-19 pandemic of 2020.

Thank you to my brother Ananda Perera, who aways cooked a feast for our families. His cooking gave me the chance to take photos to be included in my  cookbooks.

A big thank you to my book designer Alexey Lavrentev of PhotoMagLab in Ukraine. His tireless efforts and creativity made it possible for me to publish this collection of  authentic recipe books.

Above all, I'm eternally grateful for and thankful to my family: Manjula, Michael, Mikaile, Manjari, Mychal, Charith, Tracy, Ari, Suren, Diana and Freddie. You have always given me a reason to take the next step forward.

Shyamali Perera was born in Colombo, Sri Lanka, and emigrated to the United States in 1989 during Sri Lanka's civil war. She was an educator of young children for thirty years in Orange County, California. Her first book "Curry & Rice," was published as a Mother's Day gift in 2007, and was later published as an eBook in 2014. Presently she lives with her family in Southern California and continues to dedicate her time to, writing a variety of cookbooks and children's books.

www.ingramcontent.com/pod-product-compliance
Lightning Source LLC
Chambersburg PA
CBHW042133030726
47599CB00002B/454